Written by Brigitte Coppin
Illustrated by Jean-Marie Poissenot

Specialist adviser:
Mike Chrimes,
The Institution of Civil Engineers

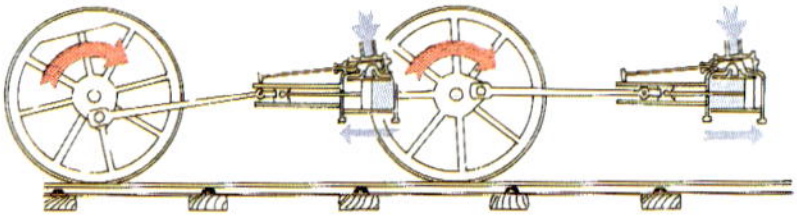

ISBN 1 85103 149 9
First published 1992 in the United Kingdom
by Moonlight Publishing Ltd,
36 Stratford Road, London W8
Translated by Sarah Gibson

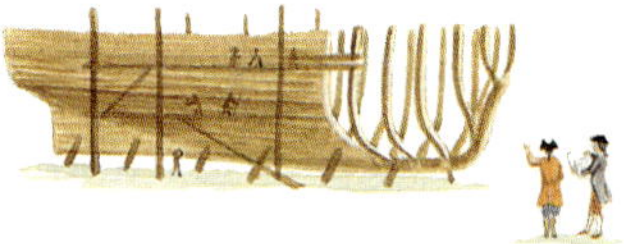

Printed in Italy by Editoriale Libraria

POCKET • WORLDS

Transport
yesterday and today

On horseback, by wagon,
by boat, by plane...

THE HUMAN WORLD

From earliest times, people used the speed and strength of animals to help them travel more quickly and move objects more easily. Early people rode horses several thousand years before wheels were made.
About 4,000 years ago, the wheel was invented. It was a breakthrough in the history of transport. Soon there were carts and wagons, later coaches, bicycles...
People built boats to travel over water, and made sails to catch the wind.
But up until about two hundred years ago, there was no machine that could do the work of the muscles of men and animals, or the power of water and wind.

Following Papin's famous steam boiler, another Frenchman, Joseph Cugnot, invented the first three-wheeled steam car in 1769.

The 18th century saw a revolutionary new invention: a machine that was powered by steam. When water boils, it turns into steam. It is possible to confine the steam in a boiler, then let it escape under pressure through a valve. The force of the steam drives a piston in a cylinder, and the movement can be transferred to wheels by connecting-rods.
One of the first men to think of using steam in this way was the Frenchman, Denis Papin (1647-1714). It was Thomas Newcomen (1663-1729), from Dartmouth, who first developed an efficient steam engine which was to play a major part in the Industrial Revolution.

A connecting-rod is jointed. It transforms the vertical movement of pistons into the circular movement of wheels.

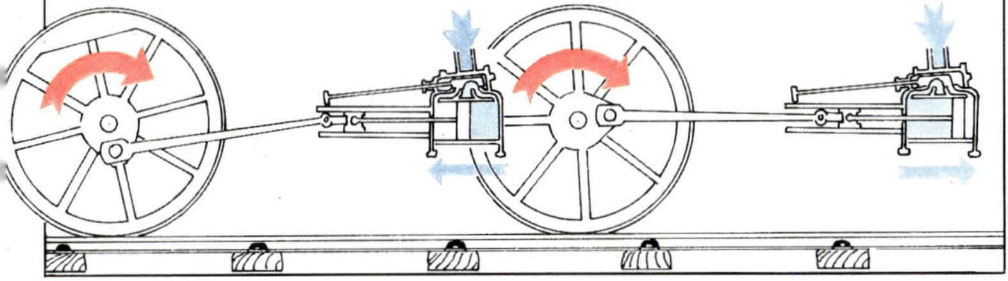

The first car with an internal combustion engine to go on sale.

Today's fuel is no longer steam, but petrol.

You had to carry a lot of water and wood or coal on board to provide enough fuel for steam-driven machines. It was a very cumbersome business! **Most modern engines are internal combustion engines.** They run on petrol or diesel, which are both products of petroleum.

**The explosion pushes the piston down the cylinder.
The piston drives the crankshaft which turns the wheels.**

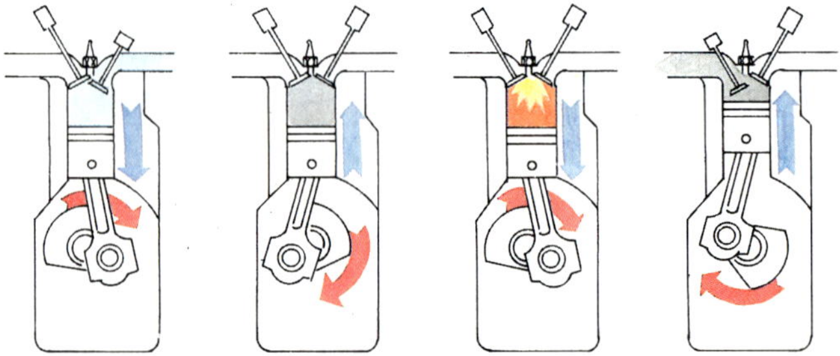

What happens inside the engine of a car?

A spark ignites a mixture of air and petrol compressed inside a cylinder, producing an explosion. This pushes the piston down, turning the crankshaft which drives the wheels. Waste products from the fuel are forced out through the exhaust-pipe. The exhaust contains a dangerous gas called carbon monoxide.

Diesel engines take their name from a German engineer, Rudolf Diesel.

At the beginning of the 19th century, the first steam locomotives were used to transport coal.

George Stephenson (1781-1848) is often called the 'father of the railway'.
He was a British engineer, who built the world's first public railway for steam trains from Stockton to Darlington.
The famous Rocket locomotive won a prize in 1829 for the best-designed steam engine. It could travel 47 k.p.h., faster than a horse could gallop.
Before long, railways were spreading across the countryside. Many men worked to keep the trains running: engine drivers and stokers, signalmen to guide the trains and station masters to look after the stations.

One of the earliest trains. The first carriages looked like stage-coaches running on rails.

On 15th May 1869 the United States of America were crossed by train for the first time. A steam locomotive used ten kilos of coal and one hundred litres of water for every kilometre it travelled.

Nowadays, there are so many trains running that they have to be organised by computers.

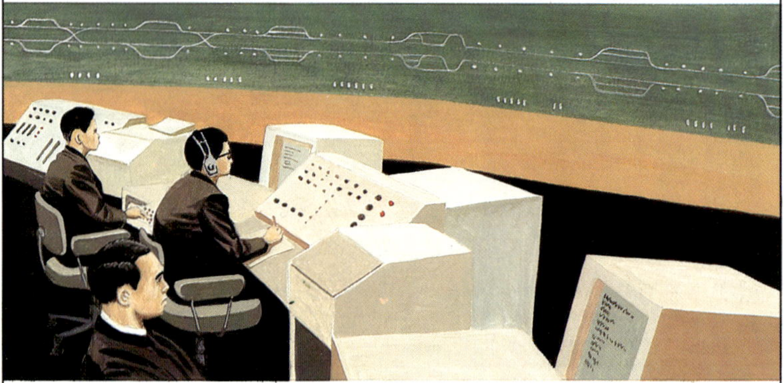

To avoid accidents, the tracks are controlled by signalmen. There are coloured signal lights at intervals along the track.

Going in and out of stations, trains are guided by a system of points. These are regulated electronically from a signal-box.

Why do trains always drive on the left?

The answer lies back in British history, long before the invention of the railway. When two knights passed in a narrow, high-banked lane, they would each keep to the left so as not to knock their swords. In many countries the first railway builders were British, and the practice of keeping to the left has been adopted all over the world.

How is a railway track built?

First the ground is spread with ballast, a bed of granite chips which will deaden the vibrations of the rails. Then heavy wood or concrete sleepers are laid over the top. The rails themselves are made of steel. They are fixed to the sleepers which keep them absolutely firm.

On an express line, the rails are welded together to give a smooth, even ride and to reduce noise and wear and tear.

Almost all urban trains are electric. Some, like this one, are fully automatic, and are controlled by computer.

This experimental train, the 'Maglev', is kept in the air by electric magnets, so there is no friction or wear on the rails.

1

2

A funicular (1) and a rack train (2) can climb steep gradients.

Trains carry both passengers and goods.
The locomotive engine is very powerful, and a freight train can be made up of many different kinds of trucks: tanks for oil or chemicals, refrigerated containers for deep-frozen products, open wagons for new cars, or closed trucks. All the goods are collected together in a marshalling yard before being sent off all over the country.

On main routes, trains run on electricity. The power is either sent along an overhead cable and through a pantograph fixed on the roof of the engine, or through a live third rail, where it is picked up by the train's collector shoes.

The fastest train in the world is the French TGV.

125
26
10

◄ The first race for cars took place in July 1894 between Paris and Rouen in France. The winner reached an average speed of 18.67 k.p.h.!

To get the engine started, you had to turn a crank handle at the front of the car before sitting down ► at the steering wheel.

The first cars were called automobiles.

The word means a vehicle that can move by itself, and it was invented in 1866, the year the first car with an internal combustion engine was built. This car had three forward gears, it could also go backwards in reverse gear and its wheels were trimmed with inflatable rubber tyres. There was no roof and no windscreen. The drivers got soaked whenever it rained, and any lady brave enough to go for a drive in one was considered a great sport! The cars often broke down: they were unreliable, and only the people who had built them were able to repair them!

1854 1910 1924 1935 1990

Articulated lorry (38 tonnes)

Steam-powered lorry (5 tonnes)

A car does not need rails.
Its tyres give it freedom of movement.
Roads are surfaced with tarmac, an oil-based product, and gravel. Even the most isolated houses and hamlets can now be reached by road or track.

The first bus, built in 1885, could carry 8 passengers.

A modern coach

But now there are too many cars on the roads! The traffic jams which clog up our cities are a waste of time and money, and contribute to air pollution.

In many countries, cars drive on the right hand side of the road.

The descendants of early hot air balloons (1) were airships that could be steered. In 1919, the Zeppelin (2) crossed the Atlantic.

1

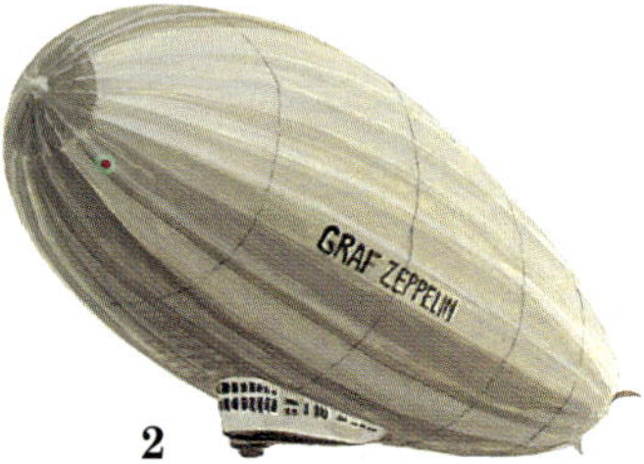

2

The first flying machines looked more like bats than birds!

At the turn of the century, people were starting to look to the sky as well. Flying was a sport which men pursued enthusiastically, risking their lives in the most unstable contraptions made of canvas and wood, held together by wire.

Clément Ader making the first powered take-off

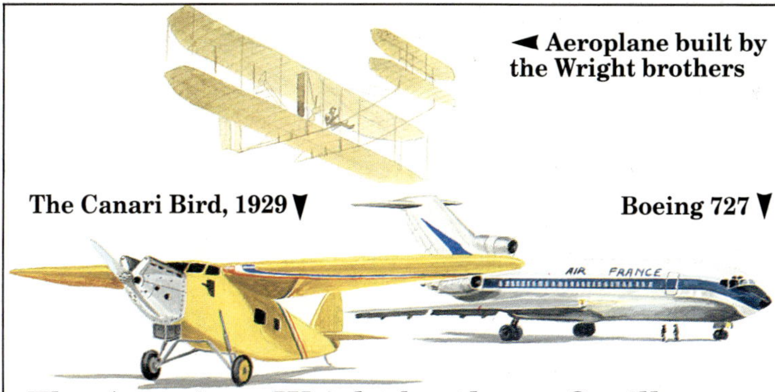

◄ Aeroplane built by the Wright brothers

The Canari Bird, 1929 ▼

Boeing 727 ▼

The American Wright brothers, Orville and Wilbur, made the first historic flight in 1903. Six years later, in 1909, Louis Blériot, a Frenchman, managed to fly over the Channel. In 1927, the American Lindbergh crossed the Atlantic by air in thirty-three hours, thirty minutes. The conquest of the skies had begun.

AIR CANADA

Small aeroplane
with propellers

◄ Helicopter

Microlight

How do aircraft fly?

Their speed and the shape of their wings keep them in the air. The difference in air pressure above and below their wings gives them lift.

Jet aircraft have extremely powerful engines. The turbojet sucks in cold air, heats it up by burning fuel, then shoots it out from the back at enormous speed. That is the white vapour trail that you sometimes see in the sky.

Helicopters do not have wings. Instead they have blades which spin at a very high speed. They can hover or land almost anywhere, even on a mountainside or a rooftop.

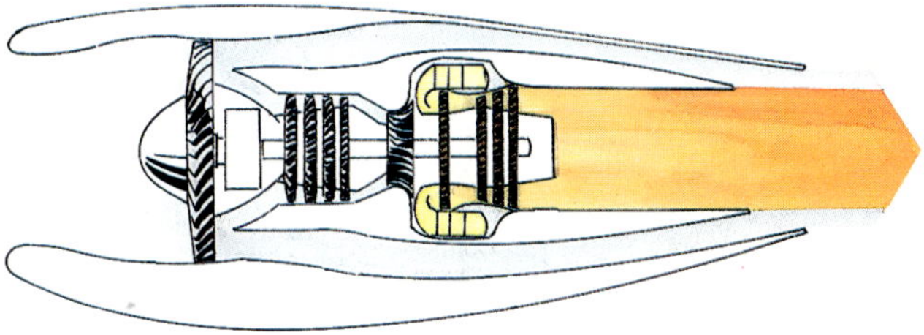

By shooting the air out from behind,
the turbofan propels the aircraft forwards.

Early aircraft were mostly used for carrying mail.

There's a highway code in the air as well as on the road!

About 12,000 aircraft take off and land every day in Europe alone.
In order to avoid accidents, they fly in air corridors.

Cargo planes are designed for carrying goods: food, machinery and weapons.

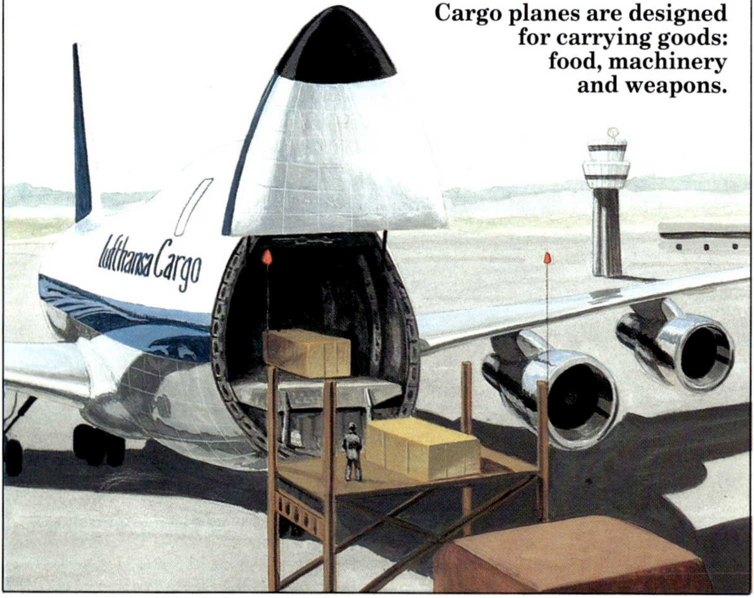

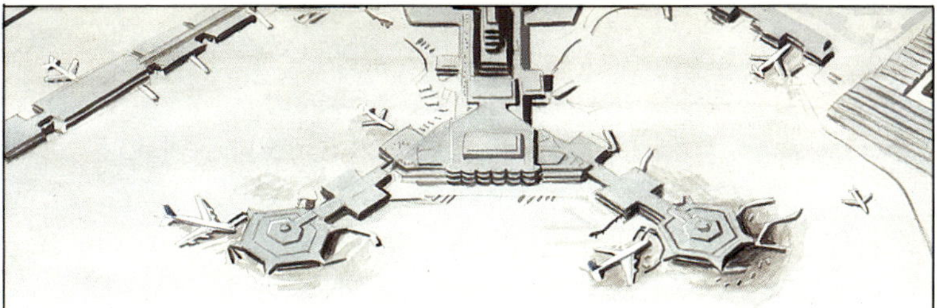

An airport seen from the air

If two aircraft are using the same corridor, they must leave a space at least six hundred metres high between them. Before take-off, the pilots make a flight plan: they choose the route they will follow depending on weather reports, the distance they have to go and the altitude of the flight.
All aircraft are tracked from the ground by radio or radar.

At the approach to an airport, air traffic controllers in the control tower guide the pilots to the runway.

In the old days, boats were built of wood. They were put together on shore by shipwrights, before being launched into the water.

Have you ever been on a sailing ship?

The wind fills the sails and pushes the boat through the water. People have known how to sail for thousands of years – crossing the oceans to trade and explore.
But what happens when there is no wind?
Almost two centuries ago, steam engines began to take the place of sails on the largest ships. First they were built with a paddle wheel, then with an engine and propellers.

The great sailing ships are long gone.

Their names still have a romantic ring: barks, brigs, schooners and clippers, some were huge ships with three or even four tall masts. They carried explorers to far-off lands and returned with cargoes of tea, spices, silks…

The hydrofoil skims the surface of the water. Its foils cause little resistance, so it can travel at high speeds.

Other giants came to take the place of the sailing ships: ocean liners.

Some of their names are still famous. At the beginning of the century, the *Mauretania* crossed the Atlantic in just five days thanks to her powerful engines. It was claimed that the *Titanic* was unsinkable, but she went down on her first voyage in 1912. These grand old ocean liners were like floating cities.

Huge propellers help the ship to push through the water. They are linked to the rudder.

Over one thousand passengers could be carried on board a liner, and there were hundreds of galley crew, waiters and cabin staff to look after them, as well as all the men needed to operate the ship. Life on board ship was in a world of its own!

Nowadays, even the largest ships can be handled by just a dozen men. They maintain radio contact with land, and they are kept informed of their exact position in the ocean by satellite. They use radar to locate other vessels and to find out the depth of the water. An automatic pilot has replaced the man at the helm.

Today, most ships are built of steel. The different parts are assembled by computer.

Some oil tankers are as long as a sky-scraper is tall.

They can transport over five hundred thousand tonnes of oil in their holds. Special docks have been built to receive them!

Heavy materials, and objects that are too bulky to go by air, travel on board cargo ships. They are stowed away safely in water-tight containers.

A lock allows boats to pass from one water level to the next. It is a section of waterway cut off by two sets of sluice-gates. When either set of gates is opened, the water level changes accordingly.

Atomic cargo ship: atomic energy heats water to drive the steam turbine engines.

In port, cranes unload the containers directly onto waiting railway trucks or lorries.

Barges are long, narrow boats.

They too transport heavy freight, such as grain or minerals, but along canals and rivers. The goods on board must not be perishable as barges cannot move fast. But they do not use very much fuel, so they are a cheap form of transport.

Have you ever seen a train of barges? Enormous barges are linked together and pushed along by a huge pusher at the back. Each barge can carry up to 1,000 tonnes.

A barge lift

Pipelines carrying gas and oil are made of steel tubes welded together. Some of them are so long that they cross whole continents.

We must not forget that some methods of transport do not move at all!

Vast pipelines carry oil for hundreds and thousands of miles, from one country or continent to another. Electric cables bring electricity from power stations to our towns and cities. Telegraphic cables lie on the ocean bed, carrying communications all around the world.

None of these has wheels or an engine, but all are means of transport nonetheless…

There is another type of transport that is quite invisible: communication!

Think of things we use every day, like the radio and the television, as well as the telephone, the telex and the fax machine.

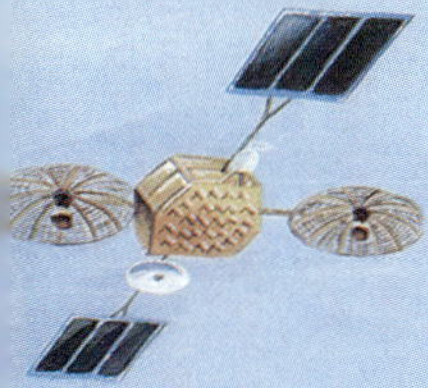

Messages are sent in the form of waves, from relay stations with powerful aerials, or via satellites, which enable news to travel from one side of the world to the other in a moment.

Without them, news would take days to reach its destination.

Telecommunication across the globe is made possible by satellites. They receive the waves, and send them back to the other side of the world.

Index

Pocket Worlds – building up into a child's first encyclopaedia:

The Natural World

- The Air Around Us
- The Sunshine Around Us
- The Moon and Stars Around Us
- Our Blue Planet
- Coast and Seashore
- Mountains of the World
- Volcanoes of the World
- Deserts and Jungles
- Rocks and Stones
- In the Hedgerow
- The Life of the Tree
- Woodland and Forest
- The Pond
- Fruits of the Earth

The Animal World

- Prehistoric Animals
- The Long Life and Gentle Ways of the Elephant
- Big Bears and Little Bears
- Big Cats and Little Cats
- Cows and Their Cousins
- All About Pigs
- The Horse
- Monkeys and Apes
- Crocodiles and Alligators
- Whales, Dolphins and Seals
- Wolf!
- Bees, Ants and Termites
- Caterpillars, Butterflies and Moths
- Birds and Their Nests
- Wildlife Alert!
- Wildlife in Towns
- Animals in Winter
- Animals on the Move
- Animals Underground
- Animal Architects
- Animal Colours and Patterns
- Teeth and Fangs